Cardiff City through the years

LORD NINIAN CRICHTON STUART.

Lord Ninian

By Annis Abraham Jnr

5th June 2009

www.annisabraham.co.uk

First pubished in June 2009 Annis Abraham Jnr.

Copyright © 2009 Annis Abraham Jnr.

ISBN 978-0-9561339-2-2

Printed by MWL Print Group

CONTENTS

www.annisabraham.co.uk

Ninian Park Cardiff Wales

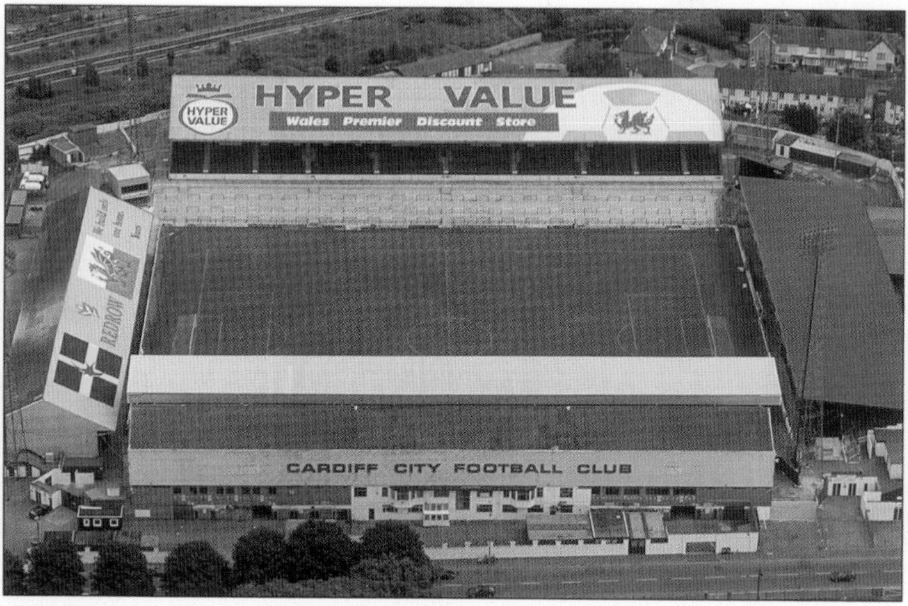

Acknowledgements

I would like to thank my Wife Joanne and Daughters Annaise & Alexandra for their input in this book and once again especially for their patience,whilst I spent hours on the internet and travelling to get the many photos in this book. They are the Love of my life and with them behind me, they have helped change my life.

To THE GRAND OLD LADY "NINIAN PARK" FOR SOME OF THE BEST MEMORIES OF MY LIFE "THANK YOU".

A special thank you to Owain Davies from Cardiff who Designed the front and back cover.

To all the staff at Cardiff City AFC, especially Peter Ridsdale(for letting me use the club badge and opening Ninian Park up to me),Julian Jenkins(Media Manager), Mona Sabbuba(Ticket office Manager), Helen Jackson(Manager of club shop) and Jason Turner(Club Secretary) .

Peter Thomas and Wayne Critchon(CCFC Photographers).
Alex Skibinski(Free lance Photographer).

Dave Sugarman(TLG), Jamie Sullivan, Steve Sullivan(Suggs), Cheggers(Blue Chegg), Jeff Marsh, Dai Camera, Jerry(Gazza), Mikey Dye, Jeff Lee(Joff), Lyndon Cushion, Wayne(aka Dibbs) & Morgan Anderson , Conrad, Glenn Villis , Gwyn Davies, David Clutterbuck, Greg(Mr Davies), Vince Alm, Paul Corkery , Tony Jeffries, Martyn Tobin(Cardiff 74) and Simmo.

Also Chris Moore & Luise Silva at Bar Zync Mill Lane, Cardiff City Centre.

My Godsons Connor Sullivan and Daniel Evans.

Snibs, Sticky and Mr Williams for 8 years of laughs in Sect A.
To Everyone from Section A of The Grandstand Upper and Lower they were Great Times "BLUEBIRDS"

Mike Morris Cardiff City unofficial website, www.cardiffcitymad.co.uk
The Valley Rams website www.valleyrams.co.uk
London Eye CCFC website www.ccfclondoneye.co.uk
Andrew Turton, The Thin Blue Line Fanzine.
Nick & Richard, Watch The Bluebirds Fly Fanzine.
Chris O'Brian website www.ccfcsleepinggiant.com

Rob, Dave and Angie at Express Imaging 172-174 City Rd, Roath Cardiff. Cardiff City Supporters Club(Vince Alm), 1927 Supporters Club (Matt, Thames Valley Bluebird), Maesteg Supporters Club, Valley Rams Supporters Club, Cardiff City London Eye Supporters Club(Helen Thomas, Sandham &Guff), Bluebirds Down Under Supporters Club, The Holyhead Supporters Club, Northern Bluebirds Supporters Club, Exile Bluebirds Supporters Club, Scandinavian Bluebirds Supporters Club and Shamrock Rovers Supporters Club.

All of the following places stock all my books Mark Dudden News agents 80 Albany Rd, Roath Cardiff. Cheggers at The Brunswick Pub, 5 Church Street, Merthyr Town Centre. Sam at A2 Clothing Victoria Street, Merthyr Town Centre. Billy Badges Stall. Sean at Cardiff Market, Sports Stall, Cardiff City Centre. Here's News 32 Albany Rd, Cardiff. Phil Southal(Referee) at Forget me not Card Shops 26 Caroline Street, Bridgend & 87 Station Rd, Port Talbot. Wayne Critchon at Ton Tan 44 Mill Street ,Tonyrefail. Cara at Quick Snack News, Caerphilly Train Station, Caerphilly. Karam at The 1927 Café(Country Kitchen) 122 Cowbridge Rd, Canton, Cardiff. Paul at Mojo King Wellfield Rd, Roath Cardiff . Dave Roberts (Newport County Fan) at Icon Computer Shop, 26 Malpas Rd, Newport NP20 5PA , Mathew Hegarty at The Loft Casuals Shop, 43 Holton, Barry Town Centre and of course at www.annisabraham.co.uk

Paul Came, Camelot Books(Wholesalers) Camelot House, Cae Glas Rd, Rumney, Cardiff CF3 3JU.

This book and From Shattered Dreams to Wembley Way are also available at Cardiff City's Club Shop.

www.annisabraham.co.uk

Introduction

The first thing I would like to say is how unique our fans are and I am not saying that because I am a Cardiff fan, I am saying this because after over 35 years of our club, always being in the doldrums and many a year in the Dungeon division (4th Division), Cardiff City fans have stuck with our club and kept on smiling/singing and have cheered on the Bluebirds from Darlington away, all the way to Wembley in 2008.

I was seven years old when I first saw Cardiff City play at Ninian Park in 1973, with a crowd of only 9,606, I was there to witness a goal by Gill Reece in a one nil victory. That day I stood on the Bob Bank, with My Grandfather Fred and when we scored it was like City had won the F.A.CUP and I was hooked. And still to this day when City Score our fans celebrate like we have won a trophy..

I have watched City through the very bad days right up to some sensational days. I have so many memories of the matches I have seen at Ninian Park, that I could write a book on just them. Beating Hereford Utd 2-1 in the old third division before 35,501 in 1976 was a night never to be forgotten. Ninian Park was jammed to the rafters and many have said, there was more like 45,000 fans in Ninian. The last minute equaliser by John Buchanan in 1980 against the Jacks was a match I will never forget. I was standing on the corner of the Bob Bank(Grange end),ready to leave at the final whistle, the Jacks were celebrating thinking they had won 3-2, when Buchanan volleyed a thunderbolt right into the net. Twenty thousand fans of the 21,198 including myself went mental as though we had won the game. There were many sad nights, like the night we lost to Luton Town 3-2, Luton had already won the old second division, so they had nothing to play for, where as if we had won, we were guaranteed to stay up, well like I said we lost and were relegated. For over ten minutes after the game had finished, I stood on the Bob Bank with tears in my eyes, like many other City fans from the crowd of 10,277, in disbelief, but that was City all over and still is right up to us loosing at Sheffield Wednesday on the 3rd May 09, 1-0, with Wednesday having nothing to play for and City just needing a draw to secure the play offs.

On a brighter note, beating the mighty Leeds Utd at Ninian Pak on the 6th January 2002, 2-1 in the F.A.CUP 3rd Rd, will rank as one of my greatest moments at Ninian Park, as they were top of the Premier League at the time and we were in my eyes in the 3rd Division(what we use to call it), and to go one nil down and then to come back and beat them ,was something I will never forget, especially when a home grown youngster from the Valleys scores the winner , "Scott Young".

I have supported City at places like Port Vale and seen us loose 6-1 and then cheered George Wood (goal keeper) off the pitch, we have lost 7-1 at Luton Town and still we have sung and danced on the terraces. So to be a City fan you have to be unique.

Ninian Park, "The Grand old Lady" is no more, and I am not ashamed to say I have shed a few tears, knowing I will no longer be able to see my Bluebirds play there, after 36 consecutive years of having a season ticket, Ninian Park became my second home and I like many other City fans shall never forget her. I really hope this book can bring back a few happy memories of your visits there. The crowds over the years have been as low as 1,510(1987 v Hartlepool) and have also been as high as 57,893 (1953 v Arsenal). What I would like to say is, in her last season the old lady had virtually a full capacity (home section) for every one of her last league games.

Over the years the media has always put Rugby first, but finally they have started to realise that our club Cardiff City has the biggest support of fans, than any other sport in Wales week in week out. I have been away with City with as little as 11 fans (1996 Gillingham away) and with 37,000 fans (to Wembley 2008),You can never forget those memories.

After the Success of my last 3 books, I decided that my latest book should be something totally different as during the last year I had noticed continuously what virtually every supporter had done when they had my books in their hands ,the first thing they would do is look for the photos and spend the next 5 minutes studying them. Also I will never forget after Shattered Dreams came out a fan called Martin (Cardiff 74 on Mike Morris message board) put on the message board how happy the book had made him and his son, that they could see themselves in one of the photos. So I looked through my collection of books on Cardiff City and saw that there had never been a fans book.

Over the last 7 months I have asked on all the football message boards for photos of Cardiff City fans and at the same time Peter Thomas (CCFC Photographer) and myself have taken many photos of City fans at the matches. I have had a great response and I have put virtually every photo that has been sent to me in my book.

The book contains photos from as early as 1910, when Ninian park was first built, right up to the last ever match played there in 2009. There are many photos of our fans, from doing the Ayatollah, watching City at Ninian Park to following our club abroad. Many fans have had tattoos of City and have kindly let me put them in the book. Some of our promotion seasons are also featured in the book. City fans following Wales abroad are also featured. I have also tried to show the fashion culture over the years, especially through the 80s, where hardly a scarf was worn, to fancy dress at many of our promotion parties and to the present where most fans now wear their City top with pride.

I am not a photographer and was never a collector of photos, so I have had to rely on you the fans for the photos in this book.

I have included 3 of our chairmen Steve Borley, Peter Ridsdale and Sam Hammam as without them, we probably would never be where we are today. Some of the staff behind the scenes are also featured, from the ticket office staff, club shop staff to people like Julian Jenkins, Wayne Critchen and Ali our famous Tannoy announcer.

I have deliberately kept the text to a minimum, as for me the pictures tell the story.

I really do hope these photos can bring back some great memories of following our beloved club, especially at Ninian Park. A new stadium lies ahead and "The Grand Old Lady" will be a fond memory for all of us, which I am sure we will never forget.

Annis Abraham Jnr   5th June 09.

www.annisabraham.co.uk

Chapter 1
The Early years

Cardiff City 1910

Cardiff fans 1910

Cardiff v. Swindon 1910

Cardiff City v. Kettering 1911

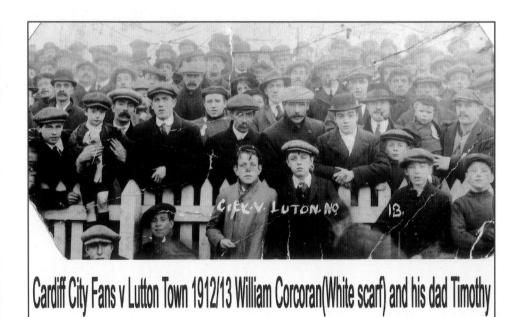

Cardiff City Fans v Lutton Town 1912/13 William Corcoran(White scarf) and his dad Timothy

Ninian Park 1925

Cardiff At Wembley 1927

Ninian park 1946

Ninian Park 1949

Ninian Park 1961

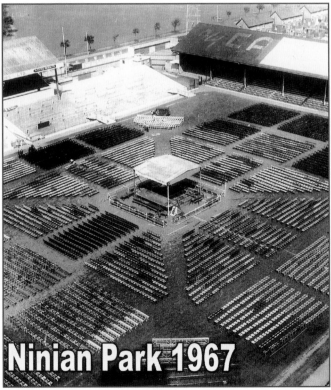

Ninian Park 1967

The Grange end, Ninian Park

Ninian Park 1998. The Ground we all love

Chapter 2
The 80s

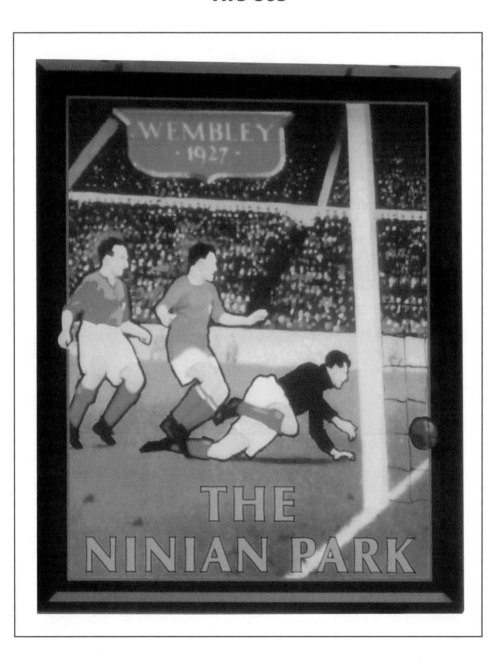

Ely Trendies in the 80's

Ely trendies in the 80's

Neath lads. The Canton stand, Ninian Park

Outside Stockports ground

Conrad, Glenn and the lads, you can't beat the 80s

The 80s, outside Cardiff Cental train station

Cardiff fans, the late 80s

Cardiff fans, the late 80s away

The late 80s

The late 80s

Newport County v Cardiff City, Cardiff fans fenced in, November 1987

Hundreds of Cardiff fans in Hereford town centre

Cardiff fans at Hereford

Caerphilly trendies 1980's

Simon and the Neath lads going away with the City

Glen and H

**The lads in the 80's
Shoulders, H, Miller,
Glyn, and Wilson**

1986 a Tuesday night at Rochdale, loyal bunch of City fans

1987, the docks and Barry boys

City fans in Brownhills pub by Cardiff train station, 1988

Brownhills pub 1988

Cardiff fans at Bristol City, away 89

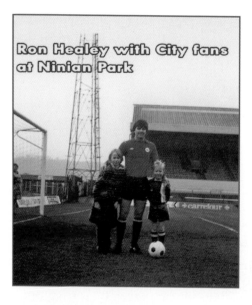

Ron Healey with City fans at Ninian Park

. NINIAN PARK ROAD
. CARDIFF
. S. WALES

DATE OF BIRTH   No.   SIGNATURE

John - True blue from Jackland 1976

THE CLAUDE

From scooter boys to city fans

Chapter 3
Our Fans

Neil Alexander with Bluebirds supporters

Lyndon, Harry and Laura
Bargoed Bluebirds

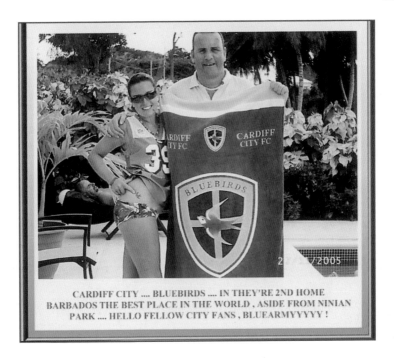

CARDIFF CITY .... BLUEBIRDS .... IN THEY'RE 2ND HOME
BARBADOS THE BEST PLACE IN THE WORLD , ASIDE FROM NINIAN
PARK .... HELLO FELLOW CITY FANS , BLUEARMYYYYY !

Kiera and Tay - True Blues

Roy Jones Taylor and Sebastian, Cardiff True Blues

Young Bluebird takes over the Liberty

Leanne, Steve and Helen

Phil and Helen Southall at Ninian Park

Charlie and Tom, Wiltshire Blues mascot for the day

A lonely Bluebird at Ninian Park

Steven Byrne and family
Bluebirds from Birmingham

A civil arrest (lol)

A diehard Bluebird, Paul and friends

Our loudest fan Dai Hunt uses his mouth and fist now he's had his drum confiscated

Cardiff fans at Ninian Park on open day

Cardiff fans at Ninian Park on open day

My wife Joanne, and the children with Santa at Ninian park. Dec 2008

Never a dull moment on Sloper Road

Ben and his friends on the Grange end

The Grange end v Spurs home

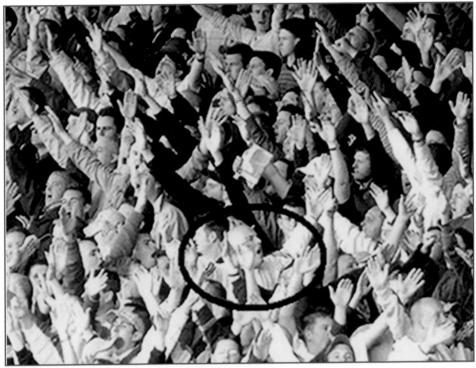

The Grange end comes alive

The Grange end, Ninian Park

The Grange end, Ninian Park

The Bob Bank, Ninian Park

The Bob Bank, Ninian Park

The valley lads house warming party

Barry casuals

Diary of the Soul Crew book launch Sept 2008
Just a few of the 700 Cardiff fans who attended

The drinks are on Mallo

Nils and Simmo with fellow Cardiff fans

Barry lads (CCFC) in their local

Cardiff V Stoke 2001

Shramrock Rover fans at Ninian Park
Sat 20.12.08 Cardiff v Sheff Wed

Cass and the Valley lads v. Forest Jan.09

Cardiff fans at Ninian Park v Arsenal, 25th Jan 09, FA cup 4th round

25th Jan 09, Cardiff 0 Arsenal 0, FA cup 4th round, Ninian Park

Arsenal Home FA CUP 2009

09/04/2009

Section A grandstand Ninian Park v Derby County, April 09

Cardiff fans at Birmingham home 2006

Marshie, Nils, Matt and Fellow City Fans

**Nash and George Cardiff 1 Birmingham 2
27 Sept 2008**

Chapter 4
The Away days

Llanelli boys going to watch Cardiff in Chester, 1975

Cardiff fans away in the early 80s

Cardiff fans away in the early 80s

Cardiff fans invade Newport in the 80s

1200 City Fans made the trip 1990

YOUNG CARDIFF CITY DEFENDER NATHAN Blake holds his head in disbelief as Cohen Griffith (left), Mark Kelly and som
Bluebirds fans applaud the supporters after Saturday's 2-0 defeat at Bury. The reverse meant City were relegated to Division Fou

Bluebirds' great escape bid is buried up north

1993 Cardiff fans celebrating winning at Scarborough 3-1

Cardiff Fans comming out of the Fulham end 1993

Cardiff Fans in the Fulham End 1993

Plymouth away 1994

Brighton 97 away

1998/99 Rochdale v Cardiff City, Div 3, loyal City fans

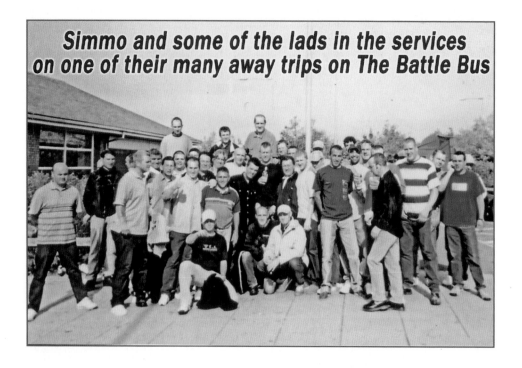

Simmo and some of the lads in the services on one of their many away trips on The Battle Bus

Cardiff fans on the train away 2006

Hull away 2006

Bristol city away 2007

The Valley Boys

QPR AWAY

Crewe away

Cardiff lads in London

Forest away

Crewe away

Cardiff City fans away in their thousands

7th Jan 06 Arsenal 2 Cardiff 1
Last ever FA Cup game at Highbury

On a cold Tuesday night in December away to Blackpool
a group of loyal bunch of City Diehards, 2007

City fans at Paddington

Bridgend Bluebirds on there way to Jack land, 23rd Sept 08

Cardiff fans at Swansea, 23rd Sept 08

City fans once again away in their thousands

Port Talbot Bluebirds

Happy days

Port Talbot Bluebirds

Young Bluebirds at Blackpool v Cardiff City 1-1

*7,500 Cardiff fans at The Emirates Stadium Arsenal in the FA cup replay
on a cold midweek night. Sadly the team lost 4 nil, February 2009*

*7,500 Cardiff fans still cheering on City as we were
being hammered 4 nil by Arsenal*

21 FABIANSKI	HEATON 13
3 SAGNA	McNAUGHTON 2
5 TOURE	RAE 4
8 NASRI	PURSE 5
9 EDUARDO	BOTHROYD 8
10 GALLAS	PARRY 11
12 VELA	JOHNSON 12
15 DENILSON	LEDLEY 16
17 SONG	KENNEDY 21
26 BENDTNER	BURKE 29
40 GIBBS	McCORMACK 44

ARSENAL **0** EBEL 36:39 **0** CARDIFF CITY

Matt Giggsy at Bristol City away
Cardiff score in last minute to equalise 1 - 1
March 09

Dibs tours Norwich away March 2009

Palace away 09
The Butchers Arms regulars
with Dave Sugarman

18th April 09 Preston Away just before seeing City hammered 6-0

PRINCESS OF WALES

21st April 09 Charlton V Cardiff Charring Cross

21st April 09 Charlton V Cardiff Charring Cross

21st April 09 Charlton V Cardiff London Underground

21st April 09
City score in last minute
Charlton 2 Cardiff 2

3rd May 09 Sheffield Wednesday 1 Cardiff City 0
3,500 City fans travel to witness the end of our play-off hopes

3rd May 09 Sheffield Wednesday 1 Cardiff City 0
3,500 City fans travel to witness the end of our play-off hopes

3rd May 09 Sheffield Wednesday 1 Cardiff City 0
3,500 City fans travel to witness the end of our play-off hopes

Chapter 5
The Ayatollah

The day the Ayatollah was taught to Cardiff fans at Peterborough in the 1980's

Cardiff fans at Peterborough in the 1980's learning the Ayatollah

DOING THE AYATOLLAH

STEP 1
An Ayatollah stands on the terrace wall and shouting 'AYA' to the crowd the crowd reply

STEP 2
The Ayatollah sits down, the crowd sit down

STEP 3
The Ayatollah starts beating hi head, the crowd beat their heads

The new way to travel to away games

CHEERS Soccer fans at the Cross Keys in St David's Road, Neath Bluebirds 2002

SNAPPERS SNAPPED: *Ryan Giggs with Adrian Ellis from Splott.*

Heads, it's 'Ayatollah' Gigg

Even Santa loves us

Cardiff fans doing the Ayatollah

Cardiff fans at Birmingham home, 2006

Mikey Dye and The Ely Trendies (lol) doing the Ayatollah in Butlins Minehead 2009

Gareth Hughes son doing the Ayatollah, mascot for the day,
Plymouth home 2007/2008

Chapter 6
Cardiff City Flags

Dave Sugarman flying the flag on Mt. Snowdon

CF14 BLUES
NORTH CARDIFF

CF14 BLUES
NORTH CARDIFF

One of Sam Hammam's many walks up Snowdonia

Cardiff City fans through the years

Billy and Bobby Santa Ponsa

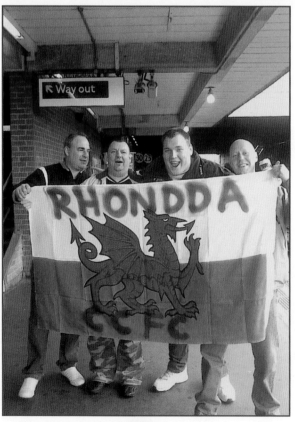

Lee, Marc and Copey
Basarah, Iraq. 2004

Cardiff and Doncaster Fans 2009

Dibs tours Norwich away March 2009

Dibs tours Norwich away March 2009

18th April 09
Preston 6 - Cardiff 0
THE FINAL WHISTLE

NINIAN PARK

In the desert in Egypt on a campsite 'Bluebirds'

Junior

Chapter 7
Cardiff City Fans Abroad

16th Sept 93, chairman Rick Wright applauding the 1200 Cardiff fans who went to standard Liege. We lost 5-2 in Belgium

We've scored but lost 5-2 in standard Liege

Cardiff Fans in Liege 1993

Standard Liege 5 Cardiff City 2, Myself and other City fans celebrating a goal.
European cup winners cup 16th Sept 93

Admira Wacker v Cardiff City (Austria)

Cardiff fans in Eindhoven November 1996

*Myself and Patrick showing the Welsh flag off surrounded
by 3000 English fans, Toulouse 1998*

Berwick Rangers v Cardiff City, pre-season Scottish tour

Pre-season friendly, Malmo (Sweden) away 2003

Cardiff airport ready to fly

Cardiff fans in Malia in a sports bar 1999

Cardiff fans in Malia on holiday 1999

*Cardiff fans in Portugal just before we beat Celtic in 2008
to win the Algarve cup*

Chapter 8
Cardiff City Fans Away with Wales

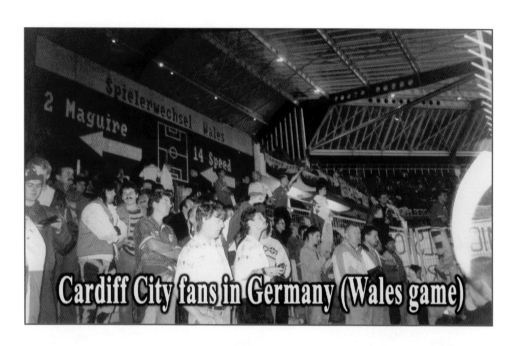

Cardiff City fans in Germany (Wales game)

Cardiff City fans in Germany (Wales game)

Cardiff fans locked up abroad following Wales in Belgium

1988 Cardiff fans in Amsterdam to see Wales

Cardiff fans in Belgium 1991

Cardiff fans in Brussels
Belgium v. Wales (1990's)

Cardiff City fans in Belgium (1990's Wales game)

Cardiff City fans in Belgium (1990's Wales game)

In Denmark, Welsh fans and Danish fans mix together, 1998

Cardiff fans 1998 in Denmark to see a rare Welsh away win

September 03 Milan
Italy 4 Wales 0

Cardiff fans in Cyprus to see Wales win 1:nil

Cardiff fans in Cyprus to see Wales win 1:nil

Budapest watching Wales beat Hungary, 2004

Mallo, Steven and fellow City fans arrive in Moscow

Cardiff fans in Norway with Wales

Matt and the 1927 Club in San Marino with Wales 2007

Cardiff Fans in Germany

**Germany v Wales 08
Frankfurt, Con's Tours**

Chapter 9
Cardiff City Tattoos

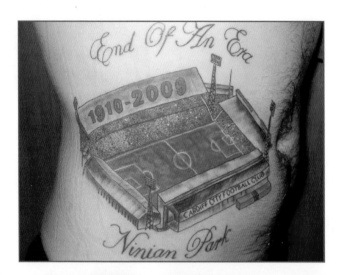

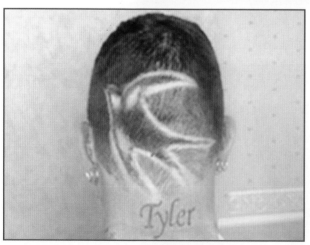

Chapter 10
The Blues are Going up

Barry Boys on their way to Burnley 7th May 1988, to celebrate promotion. Nick, Paul, Jiffy, Lenny and Obby. City won 2-1, Alan Curtis, Jimmy Gilligan

Burnley away May 1988 - The Blues are going up!
Thousands of Cardiff fans make the long trip

Burnley away May 1988 - The Blues are going up!
Thousands of Cardiff fans make the long trip

Burnley away May 1988 - The Blues are going up!
Thousands of Cardiff fans make the long trip

Burnley away May 1988 - The Blues are going up!

Thousands of Cardiff fans make the long trip

Burnley away May 1988 - The Blues are going up!
Thousands of Cardiff fans make the long trip
City win 2 - 1

1993 Cardiff fans outside the Corporation pub before Shrewsbury home game

'93 Shrewsbury Home

We're promoted! 1993

Cardiff fans celebrating promotion after beating Shrewsbury (1993)

We're going up! 1993

Darren, John and Nigel Blues promotion at Scunthorpe 1993

Cardiff fans celebrating winning Division 3 at Scunthorpe 1993

1993 Scunthorpe away, my old mate Chrissy celebrating 3 nil to City

CITY CELEBRATIONS: Nathan Blake is carried off Ninian Park by jubilant fans after the game which took Cardiff City to the top of Division Three

Cardiff fans on the way to York (in style) to see City win promotion 2001

At Hartlepool CCFC Supporters Club
Promotion year 2001

PLAY OFF FINAL CARDIFF

We're up QPR 0 Cardiff 1 May 03

We're up QPR 0 Cardiff 1 May 03

We're up QPR 0 Cardiff 1 May 03

**25th May 03 Play-off Final
Cardiff 1 QPR 0 - We're promoted!**

We're up QPR 0 Cardiff 1 May 03

Play off Final 2003
QPR 0 - Cardiff 1

Mike Morris and Nigel Blues with Andy Campbell (Scorer of the winning goal in the play off final v QPR, May 2003)

Chapter 11
Cardiff City Fans with Our Chairmen

Sam Hammam champagne army

Sam Hammam's champagne army reception, Mansfield away 2001

Sam Hammam at Brecon Beacons with Vince, Terry, Gwyn, Corky, Simon, Mogs, Kettie, Gary and Mac, summer 2005

Sam Hammam, Big Sam, Peter Morgan and fellow Bluebirds

Sam and a group of Cardiff City fans ready for a charity walk up Snowdon, summer 2006

Sam Hammam & Big Sam on one of their many walks

Sam Hammam, Peter Risdale, Paul Guy, Nida Hammam, Steve Borley 2006

Sam Hammam (The last supper),
The Holland House Hotel, Nov 2008.

Saturday June 28th 2008, 'From Shattered Dreams to Wembley Way'
book launch at Ninian Park, Peter Ridsdale and The Ant Hill Mob

25th January 09, FA cup 4th round Ninian Park before Arsenal Home game.
Christian Roberts (ex Cardiff player), Jason Perry (a legend), Steve Borley (vice chairman).
My daughter Annaise and Steve Dayo with his son George.

Peter Ridsdale, myself and Dave Jones.
Just after the takeover after Sam Hammam

Chapter 12
The Road to Wembley 2008

Cardiff fans at Chasetown, FA cup 3rd round, Jan 2008

We're on our way to Chasetown, Jan 08

We're going to Chasetown, Jan 08

We're going to Chasetown, Jan 08

The Ayatollah is going to Chasetown, Jan 08

Chasetown away, FA cup 3rd round, Jan 08

Ferndale Blues at Chasetown

FA Cup 4th round 2008
Hereford 1 Cardiff City 2

We've just scored at Hereford,
Alexandre and Annaise celebrating, True Bluebirds.
FA cup 4th round 2008

FA Cup 5th round 2008
Cardiff City 2 Wolves 0

Cardiff fans at Middlesborough FA cup 2008

Cardiff fans at Middlesborough FA cup 2008

Cardiff fans at Middlesborough FA cup 2008

Barnsley fans wanting to be Bluebirds

Cardiff City fans, Wembley 2008

Wembley 2008: Grandfather, Son and Grandson

Wembley 2008

The Ferndale Firm at Wembley 2008

Wembley 2008

Setting off to Wembley, FA cup semi-final v Barnsley (1 nil to City, 2008)

Mike Morris: I'm a happy man i've got my Wembley tickets (greedy Mike)

Lady Bluebirds at Wembley 2008 semi-final April 6th v Barnsley.
City win 1 nil (Joe Ledley)

Cardiff fans at Wembley 08

South Ruislip London, just before we catch the train for the final 8 minutes of journey to Wembley and see our beloved Bluebirds beat Barnsley 1 nil. Over 37,000 Cardiff fans have made the trip. Semi-final of the FA cup, 6th April 2008. Our dreams are becoming reality,

6th April 2008 on South Ruislip train station bound for Wembley and standing with the lone Barnsley fan before we beat them 1 nil in the FA cup semi-final. Wembley! Wembley!

Jamie, Alan, Dave, Bradly, myself, Leighton, Jock and Lyndon
a few miles from Wembley to see our beloved Cardiff at Wembley.
Semi-final April 6th Cardiff 1 Barnsley 0

Cardiff fans at Wembley April 08

Simon and Charles Williams at Wembley April 08

Cardiff City 0 Portsmouth 1, Wembley 08, FA cup final

Ant Hill Mob on their way to Wembley May 2008, with their beloved Cardiff City

Mr Davies and some of the boys from the Duke of Clarence, drinking outside a bar called Moloney's in Dollis Hill, London before the Cup final

FA cup Wembley, Port Talbot Bluebirds, May 17th 2008

FA Cup Final 08
Pompey 1 Cardiff 0

FA cup homecoming May 08

FA cup homecoming May 08

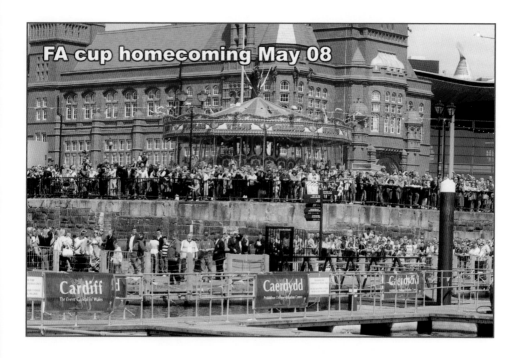

FA cup homecoming May 08

FA cup homecoming May 08

FA Cup Homecoming May 08

FA cup homecoming May 08

FA cup homecoming May 08

FA cup homecoming May 08

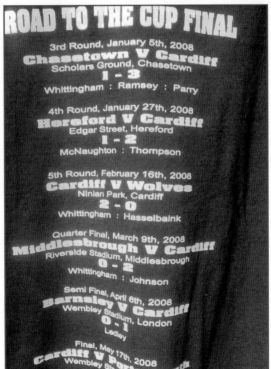

ROAD TO THE CUP FINAL

3rd Round, January 5th, 2008
Chasetown V Cardiff
Scholars Ground, Chasetown
1 - 3
Whittingham : Ramsey : Parry

4th Round, January 27th, 2008
Hereford V Cardiff
Edgar Street, Hereford
1 - 2
McNaughton : Thompson

5th Round, February 16th, 2008
Cardiff V Wolves
Ninian Park, Cardiff
2 - 0
Whittingham : Hasselbaink

Quarter Final, March 9th, 2008
Middlesbrough V Cardiff
Riverside Stadium, Middlesbrough
0 - 2
Whittingham : Johnson

Semi Final, April 6th, 2008
Barnsley V Cardiff
Wembley Stadium, London
0 - 1
Ledley

Final, May 17th, 2008
Cardiff V Portsmouth
Wembley St...

The FA cup 2008 that we so nearly had. My daughter Alexandra and myself

Chapter 13

The Last Ever Derby(Jacks) Game at Ninian Park

Cardiff v. Swansea 5th April 09
Welcome to the Jacks

**Chris Gunter with Murphy family
5th April 09 Cardiff v. Swansea, Ninian park**

**5th April 09 Cardiff v. Swansea, Ninian park
Chris Gunter with Cardiff and Birmingham fans**

Cardiff City v. Jacks 5th April 09

Cardiff v. Swansea 5th April 09 Sect. A

Cardiff v. Swansea 5th April 09 Grandstand

Cardiff v. Swansea 5th April 09 Bob Bank terrace

Cardiff v. Swansea 5th April 09 Sect. A

Cardiff v. Swansea 5th April 09 Bob Bank

Cardiff v. Swansea 5th April 09
Bob Bank

Cardiff v. Swansea 5th April 09
Bob Bank

April 5th 09, we've scored in the last seconds v the Jacks (2-2). The Bob Bank goes wild

April 5th 09, Bridgend Bluebirds after the Jack game

Chapter 14

Memories

IN RESPECTFUL MEMORY OF

JOCK STEIN

WHO SADLY LEFT FOOTBALL FOREVER

WHILST MANAGING SCOTLAND

AT NINIAN PARK

ON THE 10th SEPTEMBER 1985

FROM FOOTBALL FANS

ALL OVER THE WORLD

ON THE 20th ANNIVERSARY

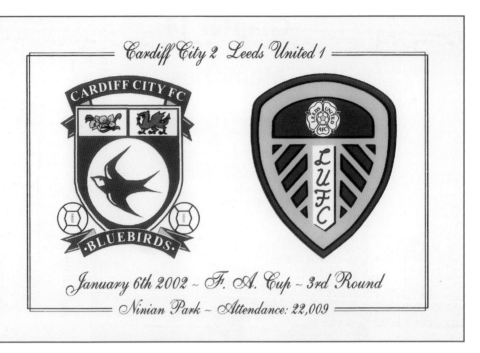

Cardiff City 2 Leeds United 1

January 6th 2002 ~ F. A. Cup ~ 3rd Round

Ninian Park ~ Attendance: 22,009

Coal Exchange Player of the year do Mark Bonner and supporters

Simmo's back garden - The Jack's home in the 1990's

City fans on TV

City fans on Soccer am

Vince Leader of the Romans
and Head of Cardiff City supporters club

Dibs Head of the
Bridgend supporters club

Dai Taxi
Ipswich away 2004
Last Game of the season

A True City fan

McNaughton sits on a jack 2008

Mona Sabbuba CCFC Ticket Office Manager and True Bluebird

25th April 09
The Ninian Park ticket office staff

Cardiff City club shop staff 2009

Gavin Davis proposes to Joanna Evans to mark the special occasion of Cardiff's last ever league game at Ninian park 25th April 09

Wayne Critchen and Darcy Blake Player of the Year presentation 09

The team who put the book together
Dave, Ang and Rob
172 City Road, Cardiff

Ali, City's Tannoi announcer and
Corky, Chairman of the CCFC supporters trust

Cheggers, Julian Jenkins (Media Manager), and myself at Ninian Park April 09

R.I.P Jeff Richards

Myself in the Cardiff City's trophy room, we haven't won a trophy for years

The 1927 Club and John Robinson at the Player of the Year Presentation

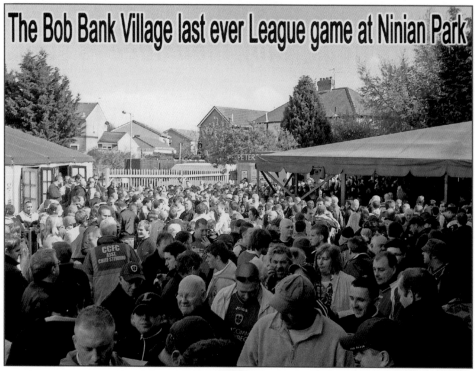

The Bob Bank Village last ever League game at Ninian Park

Last ever League game at Ninian Park 25th April 09

GRANGE
END
TERRACE

HOME
SECTION

Our famous "Billy the badge"'s stall

Our police spotter Simon enjoying 'Diary of the Soul Crew 2'

Sean's Sport stall (TRUE BLUEBIRD) Cardiff Indoor Market

Undefeated world champion, Joe Calzaghe

Match sponsors The Lads at Ninian Park in the 1990s,
Lakey, Mac, Simon, Brummie, myself, Hue, Emlyn, Patrick, Frankie and Joff.
The pre-sam years, the club was cash strapped

Chapter 15

The Last Ever League Game at The Old Lady

25th April 09
Last ever league match at Ninian Park

25th April 09
Last ever league match at Ninian Park

25th april 09
Last ever league match at Ninian Park
Cardiff 0 - Ipswich 3

25th april 09
Last ever league match at Ninian Park
Cardiff 0 - Ipswich 3

25th april 09
Last ever league match at Ninian Park
Cardiff 0 - Ipswich 3

25th april 09
Last ever league match at Ninian Park
Cardiff 0 - Ipswich 3

25th april 09
Last ever league match at Ninian Park
Cardiff 0 - Ipswich 3

25th april 09
Last ever league match at Ninian Park
Cardiff 0 - Ipswich 3

25th april 09
Last ever league match at Ninian Park
Cardiff 0 - Ipswich 3

25th april 09
Last ever league match at Ninian Park
Cardiff 0 - Ipswich 3

25th april 09
Last ever league match at Ninian Park
Cardiff 0 - Ipswich 3

25th April 09
Laura, Annaise, Alexandra and Connor
True Bluebirds !

25th April 09
Cardiff 0 - Ipswich 3

25th April 09
Dio, Chris, Jonny and Ben
Cardiff 0 Ipswich 3

25th April 09
Sect. B of the Grandstand
True Bluebirds !

Cardiff fans at the last ever League game in Ninian Park 25th April 09

Shattered Dreams

... a football club in crisis

CARDIFF CITY FC

by Annis Abraham

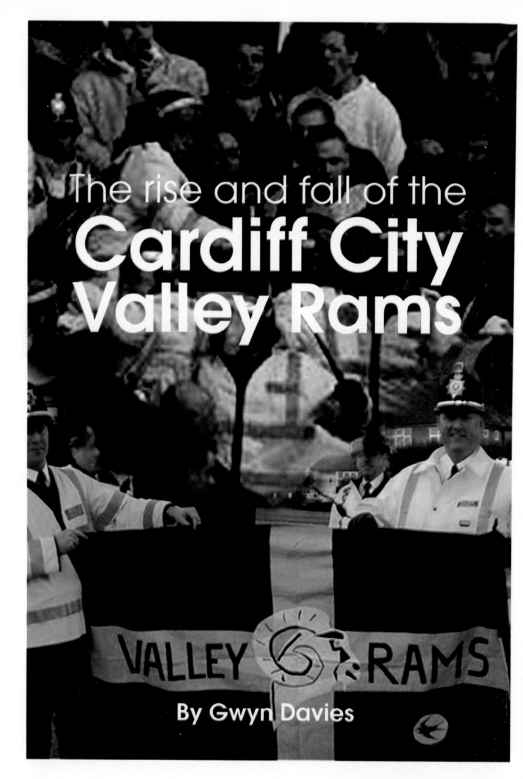

The rise and fall of the
Cardiff City
Valley Rams

By Gwyn Davies

VALLEY RAMS